# MATH FUN

## WITH
## MONEY PUZZLERS

# By Rose Wyler and Mary Elting
# Pictures by Patrick Girouard

**JULIAN ⊗ MESSNER**

# Acknowledgments

Thanks go to Joan Muzeni, River Dell Senior High School, Oradell, New Jersey for her help in the preparation of this book.

Text copyright © 1992 Rose Wyler and Mary Elting

Illustration copyright © 1992
Patrick Girouard

Published by Julian Messner,
a division of Simon & Schuster
Simon & Schuster Building, Rockefeller Center
1230 Avenue of the Americas
New York, New York 10020

JULIAN MESSNER and colophon are trademarks
of Simon & Schuster

10 9 8 7 6 5 4 3 2 1 (hardcover)

10 9 8 7 6 5 4 3 2 1 (paperback)

## Library of Congress Cataloging-in-Publication Data

Wyler, Rose.
   Math fun with money puzzlers / by Rose Wyler and Mary Elting;
illustrations by Patrick Girouard.
      p.      cm. — (Math fun)
   Includes index.
   Summary: An activities book using math to introduce the handling
of money and using money to promote math skills. Includes puzzles,
tricks, games, and jokes.
      1. Arithmetic—Juvenile literature.      2. Mathematical
recreations—Juvenile literature.      3. Money—Juvenile literature.
[1. Arithmetic.      2. Mathematical recreations.      3. Money.]
I. Elting, Mary.      II. Girouard, Patrick, ill.      III. Title.      IV. Series.
QA115.W96   1992
513—dc20
      ISBN 0-671-74313-9 (library)      ISBN 0-671-74314-7 (paper)
                                                      92-3515
                                                      CIP
                                                      AC

# Hi!

Money, money, money. People do lots of things with it besides spending it. They save it, earn it, fight over it, counterfeit it and cheat with it.

One reason so many things can be done with money is that money is mathematical. It can be multiplied, divided, added and subtracted. And that's why money leads to many puzzling problems.

Here is an assortment of puzzlers—many of them brainy, some of them zany. Try them alone first, using a calculator if you have one. Then check the answers, which are never more than a page away. And after that, try them on your friends, parents, and teachers. Show off.

You'll have fun . . . Math Fun.

Rose Wyler and Mary Elting

# TABLE OF CONTENTS

## INTRODUCTION    3

## COIN CLOSE-UPS    6

Common Cents; Hot Money; Penny Polish; Cheaper Pennies; Weight Check; Dimes and Decimals; Coin Sandwiches; In the Bad Old Days; What Good is a Counterfeit Coin?; Finding the Fakes; Blind Man's Bluff with Coins; How to Make Genuine Fake Money; The 90¢ Special; The Swiss Bank Holdup; Change, Please; The Million Dollar Question.

## DOLLAR DAZE    18

Strong Dollar; The Money Factory; Worn-out Money; Counterfeit Rip-Offs; The Silver Dollar Blooper; Money For Sale; Little Teasers; Interested in Interest?; Credit Card Deals; The Ghost Dollar; Loan Sharks.

## GET RICH QUICK—MAYBE    28

The Gold at Rainbow's End; The Wonderful Money Tree; Money by Magic; Advice to Fortune Hunters; Making Money at Sea; Can Chain Letters Make You Rich?; The Berry Pickers; Brain Ticklers; Popcorn Profits; Buddy's Businesses.

## BUY, SELL OR SWAP   40

The Manhattan Island Bargain; Skin Deal; Cow Trade-African Style; Jimmy's Used Bike Business; Making Sense Out of Percent; Profit or Loss; The President's Horse; Rounding Up, Rounding Down; Sporty Trading Cards; Price Codes; Flea Market Arithmetic

## ANYTHING WRONG HERE?    54

The Smart Idiot; Oh, O. Henry; Mike's Bike; Final Markdown; The Daughters' Quarters; The Whole Hole; The Case of the Missing Money; Pewee's Boast; Challenges,  Challenges; Arithmetrick; Golden Oldie; Tax Problem; True or False?; Strange Hardware; Weighty Matter; Big Feet, Little Feet.

## INDEX    64

# COIN CLOSE-UPS

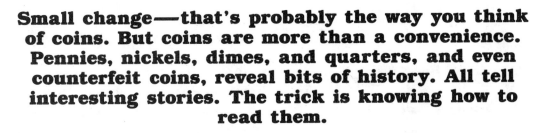

**Small change—that's probably the way you think of coins. But coins are more than a convenience. Pennies, nickels, dimes, and quarters, and even counterfeit coins, reveal bits of history. All tell interesting stories. The trick is knowing how to read them.**

## COMMON CENTS

*W*ould you believe it? No pennies are made in the United States. Strictly speaking, the coins that are 100 for a dollar are *cents*. That's the word the government uses. Round up a batch, look them over, and you'll see that each one is stamped ONE CENT.

Before the United States became a nation, small English coins called pennies were common in many of the colonies. When Americans made their own money, coins of low value were named *cents* to avoid confusion. But the old term didn't die out

and many called the new coins pennies. Most of us still do today.

Do all your pennies have Lincoln's head engraved on one side and the Lincoln Memorial monument on the other? Probably, since that's the type of cent that has been made ever since 1959. Notice the dates on your coins, then line them up from the oldest to the newest. Which one is the oldest? Can you spot any differences between the old and new coins?

As you check the dates on your pennies, use a magnifier. A magnifier will also help you see the statue of Abraham Lincoln in the center of the Memorial monument. It is tiny, but clear. On the steps you will find the initials of Frank Gasparro, the artist who made the engraving for the coin. Even though the cent is the least valuable United States coin, it is beautifully designed.

Speech bubbles:
HERE'S A VERY RARE OLD COIN FROM THE TIME OF THE ROMANS. SEE, IT'S STAMPED 59 B.C.

BUT THEY DIDN'T DATE COINS THEN DID THEY?

WELL THAT'S WHY IT'S SO RARE.

# HOT MONEY

Because of the copper in a penny, the coin can be used in a neat trick. Tell your friends you have a sense for cents. To prove it, have them put several pennies in a hat. While your back is turned, ask one of them to pick out a penny and concentrate on the date. Then have the penny passed to the others and ask them to concentrate on the date, too. When the penny is back in the hat, turn around, pick it out, and call off the date on it.

How do you do it? You just feel the pennies and find the one that is warmer than the others. Copper is a good conductor of heat, and so the chosen penny gets warmed up as it is passed around.

# PENNY POLISH

Details on your pennies may be hard to make out if the coins are dirty and dull. The dullness does not mean a coin is old. A penny that has been kept in a dry, closed space will keep its coppery gleam for years. But when exposed to the air for a while, a chemical compound called copper oxide forms and dulls the surface.

To restore the shine to your pennies, put them in a dish. Sprinkle salt on them, add a few drops of vinegar, and, in a few minutes they will shine like new.

Metal coins have been in use for more than 2,000 years. The oldest known coin was made in Lydia, a Greek state, around 670 B.C. The earliest dated coin that has been found comes from Denmark. It bears the date 1234 (MCCXXXIIII).

# CHEAPER PENNIES

*A*ll pennies contain copper, but pennies made before 1982 contain more copper than those made after that date. The earlier coins are made of a metal mixture that is 95 percent copper, while the newer coins are 97.6 percent zinc and only 2.4 percent copper. All the copper in them coats the zinc, and so they look just like the older pennies. See if you can detect any difference between them.

Why was the change in metal made? The price of copper went way up and zinc, a cheaper metal, was used in its place to save money. Pennies had been costing eight-tenths of a cent to make but when zinc was used the price was lowered to six-tenths of a cent. That difference may not seem like much—just two-tenths of a cent—until you take into account how many pennies are made each year.

The government makes coins in a factory called a mint. At the mint in Philadelphia, Pennsylvania, machines stamp out 10,000 pennies an hour. The same kind of machine makes pennies in the mint in Denver, Colorado, but they are stamped with a small D below the date. Together the mints produce 12,500,000,000 pennies a year.

Can you figure out how much the government saved in 1982 by making cheaper pennies? Since one cent was saved on every five that were made, divide by 5 to find the answer:

**12,500,000,000¢ ÷ 5 = 2,500,000,000¢**

And that was a lot of change. It came to $25,000,000.00!

# WEIGHT CHECK

*P*ennies made before and after 1982 are alike in size, but not in weight. That's because zinc is lighter—less dense—than copper. Newer pennies weigh 2.50 grams, while older ones weigh 3.11 grams, a difference of .61 grams. (One gram equals .035 ounce.)

When you handle the coins, you don't notice the difference in their weight. A good scale is needed to detect it. Is there one in your school that you can use? If not, you can make one.

**Here's how:**

1. **Twist a rubber band around a pencil several times. Then place the pencil across the center of a ruler. Bring the free end of the rubber band under the ruler, and wrap it around the pencil several more times until the ruler is held snugly beneath the pencil.**

2. **Cut a piece of thread about 20 inches (50 centimeters) long and use it to thread the needle.**

Poke the needle through a paper cup a little below the rim. Then run the needle through the opposite side of the cup.

3. Remove the needle and tie the ends of the thread together. Repeat this using another cup like the first one so that you have a loop of thread running through each cup.

4. To hang the cups, tape one loop to one end of the ruler and the other loop to the other end. Make sure the two cups are the same distance from the ends of the ruler. Rest the ends of the pencil on two chairs of the same height. Adjust the ruler until it is level. Then put a penny of the same year in each cup. If the cups balance, the scale is ready.

Now, put a pre-1982 penny in one cup and a post-1982 penny in the other one and you will see which is heavier. Will 3 pre-1982 pennies balance 4 light ones? How about 4 heavy pennies and 5 light ones?

If you had 1,000 heavy pennies, how many light ones would you need in order to balance them?

To find the answer, first get the weight of 1,000 heavy pennies:

$$3.11 \times 1,000 = 3,110 \text{ grams}$$

Then just divide to find out how many light pennies weigh that much:

$$3,110 \div 2.50 = 1,244 \text{ pennies}$$

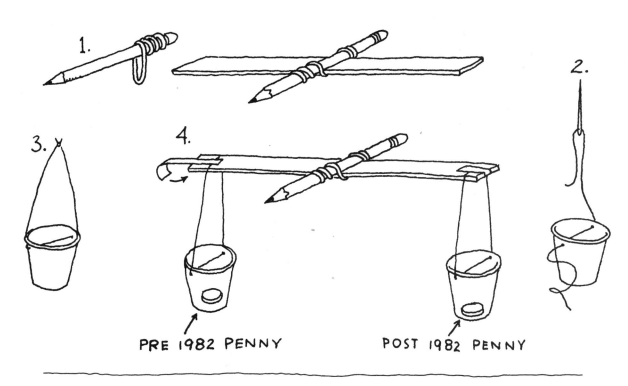

PRE 1982 PENNY          POST 1982 PENNY

# DIMES AND DECIMALS

Using your scale again, put a dime in one cup and a post-1982 penny in the other. Do they balance? They should, for each weighs 2.50 grams. But they are different in other ways.

Put a dime on top of a penny and you'll see it's slightly smaller and thinner. The metal in it is worth more than the metal in a penny. After all, a dime is worth more—ten times more, in fact.

And thereby hangs a tale.

The first dime made by the government of the new United States was called *disme,* (pronounced *deem*), a French word meaning "tenth." The name came from *La Disme,* the title of a famous book about the decimal system. Congress had chosen it because the coin was to equal a tenth of a dollar in a money system based on decimals.

A decimal money system was a new idea, and it was very popular in the new nation. In the old British money system used in the colonies, the pound was the main unit. It was divided into 20 parts called shillings, and the shilling was divided into 12 parts called pence for pennies, each worth 1/240 of a pound. A penny, in turn, was divided into 4 parts called farthings, each worth 1/960 of a pound. Compare that to the new system with a dollar divisible into 10 parts, later known as dimes, and dimes divisible into 10 parts called cents.

No wonder decimal money was popular! Now, writing sums of money was easy. As school arithmetic books explained, "Put figures for dollars to the left of a decimal point. Put the figure for the tenths of a dollar—the dimes—to the right of it, followed by the figure for the hundredths of a dollar—the cents." Recognize the method? It's the one we still use.

Since people didn't throw their old coins away, children were also taught how to change money from one system to the other. They were given problems like these:

If a pound is worth $5.00, what are 15 pounds, 10 shillings, and 6 pence worth? What is $16.25 worth in pounds? Try those problems and you'll be glad we now use decimal money.

**Answers:** $77.625 and 3 pounds/5 shillings.

# COIN SANDWICHES

*H*ave you ever noticed a coppery gleam along the edge of a dime? Copper is sandwiched between the more expensive silvery metal that coats both sides of the coin. Quarters, half dollars, and silver dollars are made in the same way.

Coin sandwiches are milled—that is, their edges are marked with fine lines. Milling was started because crooks used to shave some metal off coins, then sell the metal. The milled edges stopped that. But other ways of cheating with coins were soon found.

# IN THE BAD OLD DAYS

*T*his old saying warned people of frauds:
"Who makes it, tells it not,
Who takes it, recognizes it not,
Who recognizes it, wants it not,
So try to learn to spot a counterfeit coin."

Just the same, over one hundred years ago, many people were taken in by a coin fixed up by Josh Tatum, a counterfeiter. A new nickel had been introduced. On one side was a head symbolizing liberty; on the other, a large V, the Roman numeral for five. Tatum gold-plated a few

thousand of these nickels and made them look like the $5 gold piece then in use. He would often go to a store, buy a 5¢ item, and lay down his gilded coin. Usually, he was given $4.95 in change.

Eventually, Tatum was arrested, but a jury set him free because he had never asked for change. The case became famous and led to a new word for *joking*. This new word was *joshing*.

# WHAT GOOD IS A COUNTERFEIT COIN?

*T*his is a tale of three girls who were selling lemonade.

Sally had set up the stand and provided the cups and a cooler with ice cubes. Julie had supplied a pitcher of lemonade, and Doris

had brought the napkins. The price for a drink was 25¢. After some arguing, the girls agreed on how to divide the money from the sale. A half was to go to Sally, a fourth to Julie, and a sixth to Doris.

The lemonade was good and the girls sold all they didn't drink. They had 12 customers, who paid with quarters. But, unfortunately, one of the coins turned out to be counterfeit.

"Well," said Sally, "we'll just divide the 11 good quarters."

"But half of eleven won't come out even. Neither will a fourth or a sixth," said Julie. "What shall we do?"

"Let me handle it," said Doris. And much to her friend's surprise, she divided the coins so that each one got her fair share.

Guess how she did it.

First Doris added the counterfeit quarter to the 11 good ones. Then she divided up the 12 coins. Sally's share was a half, so she got 6 quarters—$1.50; Julie's share was a fourth, so she got 3 quarters—$.75; Doris's share was a sixth, so she got 2 quarters—$.50. A coin was left over, but that one was the counterfeit, which turned out to be useful after all.

Why did the method work? Think of the problem this way. Sally's share is twice Julie's share, and Doris's share is two-thirds of Julie's. Now if you use $x$ for Julie's share, Sally's share is $2x$ and Doris's share is $\frac{2x}{3}$. Add them and you get:

$$x + 2x + \frac{2x}{3} = 3\frac{2x}{3},$$

**and that equals $2.75**

So $x$, which is Julie's share, equals $.75; $2x$, Sally's share, equals $1.50; and $\frac{2x}{3}$, Doris's share, equals $.50.

Would the divisions work with 12 real quarters? No, $.25 would be left over—and try dividing that into a half, quarter, and sixth.

# FINDING THE FAKES

*H*ave you ever wondered how to tell real coins from fakes?

Of course, if you know the weight of a true coin, you can test suspected coins by weighing them one at a time. But suppose you have a batch of 8 coins that look alike, and you know one is a counterfeit that is slightly lighter than the others. How can you find it with just two weighings on a balance?

This puzzler is an old one. Although many people have been stumped by it, maybe you can solve it.

First try to figure out how to group the coins before weighing them. Then check your idea using a balance—your homemade scale. For coins, use 8 pennies: a post-1982 penny for the counterfeit, since it's lighter than the earlier ones, and 7 pre-1982 pennies for the true coins.

To find the answer, separate the 8 coins into groups of 3, 3, and 2. Put the coins from one group of 3 on one side of the scale and the other group of 3 on the other side. If they balance, the counterfeit coin is in the group of 2. But which one is it? Using your balance, see which coin is lighter. That one is the fake.

But suppose the groups of 3 do not balance. You know the fake is in the lighter group. So take 2 coins from this lighter group. Now try to balance the 2 coins on the scale while keeping the third in your hand. If they do not balance, the lighter coin is the fake. If they do balance, the fake is in your hand.

Sneaky, but neat. If you solved it, give yourself a medal.

# BLIND MAN'S BLUFF WITH COINS

*I*n this game you can vary the rules and make it as hard or as easy as you wish. It works best with from 2 to 4 players, and with 50¢ or more in coins of different denominations. Place the coins in a box. Besides the coins, you will need slips of paper, each with a different amount under 50¢ written on it, such as 39¢, 23¢, and so on. Each player draws a slip and, then, without looking at the box, tries to pick out the coins that equal the amount on the slip.

Coins are to be returned to the box after each trial. Let each player take two or three slips and then give fake money prizes to all who pick out the right coins.

# HOW TO MAKE GENUINE FAKE MONEY

*F*ake money is useful in lots of ways. If you have a batch, you often can work out problems with it, or check on your answers. Try handling the division of $2.75 with fake money and you'll quickly see why the girls had trouble figuring out each one's share.

To make fake money, take a cereal box and cut the cardboard into strips. Cut one strip the width of a penny, put a penny on it, and draw a circle around it. Draw another circle next to it and repeat this until the strip is covered. Cut out the circles, write 1¢ on each, and, if you wish, use your initials as a mint mark.

Nickels, dimes, quarters, and half dollars can be made the same way. Cut up a big cereal box and you'll be rich—in fake money.

# THE 90¢ SPECIAL

*T*hat's all you need for this puzzler—90¢. Try it by yourself, or make a game of it with friends.

It doesn't matter if the coins are fake or real, as long as you have 5 dimes, 4 nickels, and 20 pennies. The object is to arrange the coins in three rows of nine boxes so that they give the same sum when they are added horizontally, vertically, or along a diagonal.

That's the way numbers add up in a magic square. In the one shown, the numbers in each column, row, and diagonal add up to 15 and the total for the entire square is 45.

In tackling the 90¢ special, take some paper and draw a square divided into 9 boxes. Figure out how much money goes into each row. Decide how much goes in the center box and then figure out where the rest goes.

# THE SWISS BANK HOLDUP

*T*erry had a Swiss uncle who gave her a funny toy bank. The bank itself was a castle. Before it stood a little man aiming a gun at his son, who stood before the castle with an apple on his head. The man with the gun was William Tell, hero of a Swiss legend. The little man was rigged up to do what William Tell did—shoot an apple off his son's head without hurting him.

The toy worked like this. You put a coin on the gun, then pressed down William Tell's foot. This released a spring and shot off the coin, which knocked the apple off the boy's head, and then went into the bank. You could reload the gun and shoot coin after coin, which would knock down the apple and then

go into the bank. Pennies, nickels, dimes, and quarters could be used as ammunition.

When relatives visited, Terry would get out the bank and show them how it worked. After they shot pennies and dimes into it, Terry would slyly say, "Let's see if you can shoot in quarters." Then, zingo! One quarter after another would fly into the bank.

Terry's brother called it the "Swiss Bank Holdup," since no one ever asked for a return of the coins.

The bank soon became loaded with quarters, and Terry felt rich. But she began to wonder if she was so clever after all. If the bank was filled with quarters, would it hold more money than it would hold if it was filled with dimes? Which way would she be richer?

What do you think? Can you prove your idea is right?

If you think the bank holds more money when it is loaded with quarters, you're wrong. Dimes are smaller and fill space more completely than quarters. Quarters are worth 2 1/2 times as much as dimes, but over 3 times as many dimes fit into a container.

To check on this, take a small box, like one that holds paper clips, and fill it with real or fake dimes. Empty the box, count the dimes and figure out their value. Repeat this with quarters, and you'll find there was more money in the box when it held dimes.

Liz, do you see any change in Spot?

No, Norton. Why do you ask?

He just swallowed a dime.

# CHANGE, PLEASE

𝓕 ake money may help you answer these teasers:

1. **What is the greatest number of coins you can have and still not make change for a dollar?**

2. **What is the least number of coins that add up to 98¢?**

3. **Sid, Tom, and Boris each picked up a can of soda that cost 85¢, then each went to pay his check. Each had a total of $1: in quarters, nickels, and dimes. Sid had 3 quarters, Tom had 2, and Boris had 1. Two of the boys paid the exact amount for the soda but one needed change. What coins did each boy have and which one needed change?**

4. **Two coins in use all the time**
   **Add up to fifteen cents**
   **Yet one is not a dime.**
   **How come?**

5. **And here's a groaner. Why is a penny like a cow?**

Answers:
1. **The largest number of coins that won't make change for a dollar is eleven: 3 quarters, 4**

dimes, and 4 pennies, adding up to $1.19.

2. Seven is the smallest number of coins that add up to 98¢, and they are 1 half dollar, 1 quarter, 2 dimes, and 3 pennies.

3. Lay out $1 in change for each boy, starting with the number of quarters he had. Then make up the rest in nickels and dimes. You will find that:

Sid, who had 3 quarters, also had 5 nickels. So he didn't need change.

Tom, who had 2 quarters, also had 5 dimes. When he paid for his soda, he used the quarters and 4 dimes and got a nickel in change.

Boris, who had 1 quarter, also had 7 dimes and 1 nickel. Since he paid for his soda with the quarter and 6 dimes, he didn't need change.

The only one who didn't have exact change was Tom.

4. The coin that is *not* a dime is a nickel.

5. A penny is like a cow because it has a head and a tail and two sides.

# THE MILLION DOLLAR QUESTION

*W*hat does a million dollars look like?

If you piled a million one dollar bills, one on top of the other, the pile would be over 625 feet high, higher than a sixty-story building. Since a dollar bill is 6.0625 inches long, a million of them, placed end to end, would extend more than 95 miles!

A million dollars in dimes would be even longer. A dime is .72 inches wide, and 10,000,000 dimes make $1,000,000. They would form a line 7,200,000 inches or 600,000 feet long. Divide that by 5,280, which is the number of feet in a mile, and you get:

$$600,000 \div 5,280 = 113.6 \text{ miles}$$

Would a million dollars in quarters be longer, or shorter? Measure a quarter and you will find that it is about .96 wide. Since four quarters make a dollar, 4,000,000 quarters would be needed to make $1,000,000. To find how long a line all those quarters would make, get out your calculator and multiply 4,000,000 by .96, divide by 12, and then by 5,280.

Is your answer 60.6 miles?

As to the length of a line that a million dollars in pennies would form . . . well, measure a penny and then figure that out yourself, if you are interested.

In any case, you certainly wouldn't want to cart around $1,000,000 in pennies. The pennies would weigh over 57 tons!

# DOLLAR DAZE

**Imagine shopping with $50 in nickels and dimes, or getting $100 in quarters, for doing some work, and you quickly see what a mess we would be in without paper money. Although dollars are a great convenience, handling them creates problems . . . some of them, real teasers.**

## STRONG DOLLAR

The paper in a dollar is strong. But is it strong enough to split a pencil? This trick makes it seem that a dollar can do that.

Ask a friend to grasp each end of a pencil and hold it horizontally. Claim you will cut the pencil with a dollar bill. Hold one end of the bill with your thumb and index finger as you keep the other three fingers bent behind the bill. Then swiftly bring the bill down on the pencil, and snap! The pencil splits.

What really happens? Your friend doesn't see your index finger behind the $1. You straighten it out, then strike the pencil with it and that does the trick.

The dollar sign has nothing to do with the word dollar. That comes from thaler, the name of a German coin that was widely used in America before the Revolution. Another coin in use was the Spanish peso, written P, for short. More than one peso was written P with an s tacked on by some kind of a squiggle. When dollars replaced pesos, the simplest squiggle became the present dollar sign.

# THE MONEY FACTORY

People used to say jokingly that the company that made the most money was the American Bank Note Company. At one time, they made billions of dollars a year—that is, they printed them. They made all the legal paper money in use in the United States.

Now the national money factory is the Bureau of Engraving and Printing in Washington, D.C., which prints $1, $2, $5, $10, $20, $50, and $100 bills. These bills are called Federal Reserve Notes because after they come off the printing presses they are distributed by twelve Federal Reserve Banks to local banks throughout the country.

Examine the face of a dollar bill. To the left you will see the seal and letter of the Federal Reserve Bank that distributed it. Below that is an eight-digit serial number used to identify the bill.

The bills are hard to copy because they're made of paper containing tiny red and blue fibers that are colored with secret dyes. The fibers are easy to see. Just take a dollar bill and look closely at Washington's portrait. His face looks tattooed!

The paper used in our money is expensive. It is one-fourth linen and three-fourths cotton, which is hard to tear. At present, the cost of making any bill—$1 or $100—is $.025. That may seem high for a little piece of paper, but our money would cost much more if it were all in metal coins.

# WORN-OUT MONEY

Although the paper in our money really is strong, bills become torn, faded, limp, or too creased to be used. They are then returned to the twelve Federal Reserve Banks that distributed them. After they are counted and shredded by machines, the worn-out bills are replaced by new notes from the Bureau of Printing and Engraving.

The average life span of a $1 bill is 14 months; for a $5 bill, 2 years; for $100, 5 years. It's easy to see why larger bills last longer than smaller ones. But can you figure out how much longer a $5 bill lasts than a $1 bill? How about a $100 bill? How much longer does it last than a $5 bill?

**Answers:** A $5 bill lasts 10 more months than a $1 bill and a $100 bill lasts 36 more months than a $5 bill.

# COUNTERFEIT RIP-OFFS

Over a hundred years ago, any bank that wanted to print money could do so. Each bank used its own designs, so about 1600 banks in 34 states were issuing around 10,000 different types of bank notes.

Those days were great for criminals, for it was easy to make up a bank's name and print phony money from it. To avoid being stuck with such money, bankers used books with pictures of real and counterfeit bills. The books were updated regularly, but that didn't help much. When fake bills became known in the East, crooks would take a batch and hop a train for the West. Arriving before the updated books, they could use the fake bills without getting caught.

After the Civil War, the United States government took charge of printing bills, and passing counterfeit money became harder. But not impossible. Nowadays, great numbers of fakes turn up among the worn-out bills that go into counting machines. In just one year, 1988, the machines found

COACH CAR
WESTERN PACIFIC R.R.

over 100 million worn counterfeit bills!

Shopkeepers try to be on guard against counterfeit money but they sometimes get stuck with it, as Sam Willet did.

One day a man bought a $5 cap at Sam Willet's store and paid for it with a $20 bill. Since Sam didn't have the right change, he got change from a friend next door. Then he gave the customer the cap and $15. Later, his friend learned that the $20 bill was counterfeit. So Sam gave him $20 in good money.

Sam was sore, and no wonder. What was his total loss?

**Answer:** $15 + $20 + the cost of the cap.

By the way, ask local shopkeepers how they identify counterfeits.

# THE SILVER DOLLAR BLOOPER

From time to time, the United States government has minted silver dollars. Since the coins were quite heavy, they were never very popular. Eventually, they were discontinued, and no $1 coins containing large amounts of silver were made after 1935. Some years later, when a recession was underway, the Treasury Department, which handles our money factories, decided that $1 coins would mean great savings for the country. A study had shown that the mint could make a silvery metal $1 that would cost 3¢ and last at least 15 years. In the long run, the coin would be cheaper than a $1 bill, which then had an average life of 18 months and cost 1.8¢ to make.

In 1979 a new $1 coin appeared. It was stamped with the head of Susan B. Anthony, a famous leader in the fight for women's rights. In size and weight the coin was like a quarter—and that turned out to be a great mistake, a real blooper! When making change, people would give out "Susie B's" as quarters or throw them into highway toll machines by mistake.

No one wanted the new coins, yet millions of them were minted. Most of those that went into circulation were soon brought to banks to be exchanged for bills. After three years the coins were discontinued.

It's hard to figure out the government's total loss on the Susan B. Anthony dollar or what it would have saved if the coin had been a success. But perhaps you can figure out what each metal dollar was expected to save in the course of 15 years.

**Answer:** Eighteen months is 1½ years, or 1.5 years. Fifteen years is ten times as long, and in that time ten $1 bills would be used up. Since each paper bill cost 1.8¢, ten bills would cost 18¢. And since a metal coin that cost 3¢ would last as long as the ten bills, each coin would save 15¢ over a 15-year period.

The Treasury Department had hoped the "Susie B's" would save millions of dollars. Instead millions of them are now in storage.

# MONEY FOR SALE

Anytime you want, you can sell dollars for the money of another country. If you want to buy yen, the money of Japan, you can go to a bank and trade your dollars for them. How many yen you get for a dollar—the exchange rate—changes from time to time. One month you may get 140 yen for a dollar; a month later, you may get 147 for a

dollar. When that happens, the value of the yen goes down. You have 7 more yen to spend for every dollar you change, and so the dollar is worth more.

How much more is it worth? To say "7 more yen" doesn't mean much. A better way to put it is in terms of percent. Percent is really a fraction. To say 1% is the same as saying 1/100; 2% is 2/100; and so on. The rise of 7 yen from 140 to 147 is an increase of 7/140, or 1/20. To change that fraction into hundredths, you find how many 20s are in 100 and multiply by 1:
100 ÷ 20 = 5 × 1 = 5%. A shorter way to change 7/140 into percent is to divide 7 by 140:

$$140\overline{)\begin{array}{r} 0.05 \\ 7.00 \\ -7.00 \end{array}}$$

Well, suppose you are in Japan and you had bought yen at 140 for a dollar. A month later, you are leaving the country. You have a lot of yen left over and want to change them into dollars. Now the rate is 133 for a dollar. That means the value of the yen has gone up. By what percentage did it rise?

Did the dollar fall by the same percentage? How much did it fall?

**Answers:** When the yen goes from 140 to 133 for a dollar, it changes 7/140, which equals .05, or 5%.

Norton, you nerd! You're cutting up a dollar bill! Why?

I'm dividing it into 4 equal parts because 4 quarters make a dollar and I need change.

While the yen rose 5%, the dollar fell by a different percentage. When you bought 140 yen for a dollar, you paid a cent for 1.40 yen.

But when you sold yen at 133 for a dollar, you were selling them at 1.33 for a cent, a loss of .07 cent. That's 7/100, or 7%.

Most banks will be glad to tell you the exchange rates of different kinds of foreign money. Why not find out how the rates change from time to time, then make up problems of your own?

# LITTLE TEASERS

1. **What amount of money can be divided fifty-fifty between two persons so that one person gets 100 times more than the other?**

2. **Suppose you work in a bank and a customer wants a $63 check cashed in 6 bills, without a single one. Can you give her what she wants, and if so, what 6 bills would you give her?**

3. **The dollar is used in places near and afar, but how can you spell it without using an *r*?**

4. **A man is walking down the street and sees a counterfeit bill on the sidewalk, but he doesn't stop. Why should he get arrested?**

5. **How can you make change for a dollar using 21 coins?**

## Answers:

1. Fifty dollars and fifty cents. One person gets $50, the other gets 50¢—fifty-fifty.

2. The 6 bills that add up to $63 are:

   $50
     5
     5
     1
     1
     1
   ———
   $63

   Yes, that's the right answer, for the lady said ". . . without a single one." Well, there isn't a single one in the 6; there are 3.

3. I-T spells *it*.

4. He should be arrested because he passed counterfeit money.

5. One way to make change for a dollar with 21 coins is with 1 half dollar, 2 dimes, 3 nickels, and 15 pennies. Another way is with 2 quarters, 3 dimes, 1 nickel, and 15 pennies.

# INTERESTED IN INTEREST?

Suppose you put $10 in a bank and leave it there for a year. When you take out your money, the bank gives you $10.50. That seems like getting something for nothing, which almost never happens. How does the bank do it, you wonder.

The 50¢ extra that the bank gives you is *interest.* For every hundred cents you deposit, the bank pays you 5 extra cents. This means the bank pays 5% interest on deposits left there for a year.

Now suppose Joe Schmo needs to borrow $10. The bank will lend him the money if he pays 10% interest yearly. That means Joe must pay the bank $10 plus $1 for interest after a year.

As a result, you get 50¢ interest and the bank has made 50¢. You may think that's not a big deal. But suppose a bank is paying 5% yearly on $1,000,000 in deposits while it lends $1,000,000 at 10%. At the year's

end, all the loans plus interest are paid back. How much money does the bank gain?

Of course a bank has expenses in running its business, but if those are not counted, what is the percentage of profit it makes by paying 5% interest on deposits and lending money at 10% a year?

(Hint: The answer is *not* 5%.)

**Answers:** Yearly interest at 5% paid on deposits of $1,000,000 comes to $50,000, while 10% collected yearly from loans comes to $100,000. So the bank gains $50,000.

Since $50,000 is half of $100,000, the bank's profit rate—not counting expenses—is 50%. And that's a very high profit rate.

## CREDIT CARD DEALS

A credit card is a wonderful piece of plastic. A cardholder can buy hundreds of dollars worth of merchandise and pay for it later.

Every month the holders of credit cards get bills for their purchases. If they pay before the month ends, well and good. If not, the credit card company (usually a bank) charges them interest at 18% to 20% a year until their bills are paid.

Suppose Mrs. Feely buys a new TV for $300 on her credit card, which charges 18% a year—that is, 1.5% a month. Then she puts off paying her bill. If she postpones it for a month, the bill will be 1.5% more. Well, that's just $4.50 more. But if she waits a year, she'll have to pay 18% more, and her TV will cost her $354.

Mrs. Feely may not mind the extra cost. Yet if she went to her bank, she could borrow $300 at 10% a year, and pay $30 interest instead of $54. Either way the bank makes money. But it can make more from credit cards than from loans.

See for yourself. Find out the interest rates on credit cards and bank loans, then figure out the difference between them.

# THE GHOST DOLLAR

Chang's father put $50 in the bank for him at the beginning of January and told Chang to do whatever he wanted with the money. So Chang spent it all on video games, withdrawing money from his account four times until there was nothing left in it.

His bank book showed the date and amount of each withdrawal. It also showed the balance that was left after each withdrawal. But there was something funny

about the figures. There seemed to be an extra dollar in the account. Had the bank made a mistake?

Here was the record in his bank book:

| Date | Withdrawals | Balance |
| --- | --- | --- |
| Jan. 6 | $20 | $30 |
| Jan. 10 | $15 | $15 |
| Jan. 19 | $ 9 | $ 6 |
| Feb. 3 | $6 | $ 0.00 |

To check his account, Chang added up the withdrawals. They came to $50 and that was correct. But when he added the balances, the total was $51. When Chang double-checked his addition with his calculator, the extra dollar was still there. "It's a ghost dollar," he decided. "It's there and it isn't there."

Chang couldn't explain why the two sums were different. Can you?

**Answer:** In closing an account, withdrawals should add up to the amount deposited, but balances are just listed for a customer's convenience.

# LOAN SHARKS

L oan sharks don't live in the ocean. They're two-legged monsters who charge desperate people extra high interest rates.

Let's say a man is out of work and needs $500. No bank will give him a loan. So he borrows $500 from a loan shark at 20% interest a week—yes, a week. If he pays back $200 plus interest two weeks later and $300 the next week, how much interest does the shark get?

**Answer:** After two weeks the interest that the man pays is:

$$\$500 \times 20\% \times 2 = \$200$$

The next week the interest that he pays is:

$$\$300 \times 20\% = \$60$$

So the total interest that the poor guy pays is $260. Wow!

What if he didn't pay up?

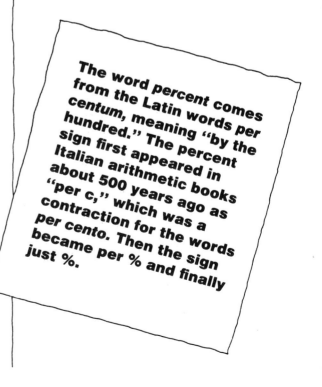

The word percent comes from the Latin words per centum, meaning "by the hundred." The percent sign first appeared in Italian arithmetic books about 500 years ago as "per c," which was a contraction for the words per cento. Then the sign became per % and finally just %.

# GET RICH QUICK — MAYBE

Easy money . . . nearly everyone would like some.
Even people with plenty of money often want more.
And this has led to many interesting dreams,
schemes, and scams. Let's look into some of them.

## THE GOLD AT RAINBOW'S END

Perhaps you know the legend of the pot of gold at the end of the rainbow. One day a farmer set out to find that gold. A big rainbow arched over his field and since he couldn't tell just where it touched the land, he dug up the earth from one end of the field to the other. Of course, he never found the rainbow's end, or the pot of gold. But his efforts were not in vain. While digging up the earth, he had plowed the land and, as a result, he had a wonderful harvest.

The moral? Don't give up. Hard work is rewarded.

And sometimes it is. But not always. Many men have mined for gold in many parts of the world, and worked very hard at it, yet only a few have struck it rich. During a gold rush, the people who outfit the miners usually make more money than the miners.

Are there any easy ways to get rich? Now and then someone has a lucky break and makes a lot of money. But people often have bad breaks too. It's easier to lose money than to make it, unfortunately.

Making money is tough business—one in which math is an important tool. No one gets rich just by using math, but, as you will see, math can help a lot.

# THE WONDERFUL MONEY TREE

Wouldn't it be great if money grew on trees? Many folktales tell of people who believed in such trees.

In one of these tales, Mountain Bill meets a stranger with a long white beard. The man said he lived on the other side of the mountain and claimed that a wonderful tree was growing on his land.

"Put money under its roots and after an hour the money is doubled. Want me to double some money for you?" asked the stranger.

Bill was an ignorant man who didn't know what double meant. But he was ready to put some of his money under the tree. When

the man wanted $3 an hour for his work, Bill almost changed his mind. So the man started to come down on his price. He finally settled for $1.20 an hour, and Bill thought he had a great bargain.

The next day Bill met the old man on the other side of the mountain. Bill gave him a purse containing 9 coins—1 quarter and 8 dimes—and then wanted to go to the money tree. But the man said, "Wait here and I'll be back with double your money."

Sure enough, the man came back with the purse. Now it contained 18 coins, and Bill let him take out $1.20 as pay for his work.

A day later Bill came back with the purse and the coins that were left in it. Again the coins were doubled and the man took out $1.20.

So Bill came back for a third visit.

Again the money that was left in the purse was doubled. But this time, after taking out his pay, the old man threw the purse at Bill and ran off. The purse was empty!

Bill never saw the old man again. And he could never figure out what happened to his money. Can you?

(Hint: Using fake money, repeat each step in the deal.)

**On trip 1:**
Bill started with 1 quarter and 8 dimes equaling $1.05.
When the money was doubled, he had 18 coins equaling $2.10.
Then $1.20 was subtracted from $2.10, leaving $.90.

**On trip 2:**
Bill started with $.90. When this was doubled, he had $1.80.
Then $1.20 was subtracted from $1.80, leaving $.60.

**On trip 3:**
Bill started with $.60. When this was doubled, he had $1.20.
And when $1.20 was subtracted from that, nothing was left.

The moral? It pays to know math.

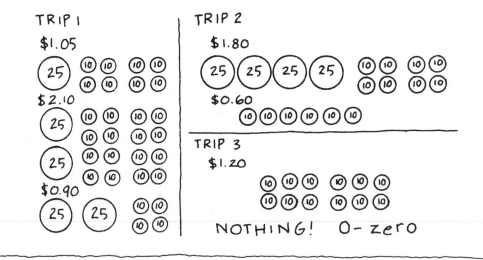

NOTHING!  0 - zero

# MONEY BY MAGIC

Today not even a small child believes money grows on trees. But a magician can make that seem possible.

The magician claims he once planted a nickel by an orange tree and now the oranges that grow on it have nickels in them.

"Here's a piece of fruit from that tree," he says, as he holds up a nice, big orange. He cuts it in two, and inside the fruit, there's a big shiny, nickel.

How did it get there? Before the trick, the magician stuck a nickel on a knife blade. When he held the knife, only he could see the nickel, and as he cut the orange, the nickel slid down into it.

# ADVICE TO FORTUNE HUNTERS

"Early to bed, early to rise, makes a man healthy, wealthy and wise."
"A penny saved is a penny earned."

Those sayings come from a yearbook called *Poor Richard's Almanac*, which was printed by Benjamin Franklin in the days of the American colonies. At the time, such sayings made sense. Workers were in great demand and those who were skilled could make a good living.

Of course, there were pitfalls. So there were sayings telling people to be cautious and avoid spending money on alluring, worthless things. A famous one was printed by Franklin. It was in the form of a rebus—a puzzle made up of letters and pictures that stand for sounds and become words when put together. Here's the rebus:

The first picture is a tool, an awl, standing for *all*; the second shows a pot of tea and stands for *t.* Can you take it from there?

Look for the answer on page 32.

**Answer to the rebus:**

The pictures on the first line—the awl, teapot, hat—read "all that." (*T* plus *hat* making *that*)

The second line with *G* plus the pigs on the straw, which stands for *litter*, plus the dog and pups makes *litter* a plural. So the line reads "glitters."

The third line with the two letters *I* and *s*, a knot in wood, and a gold coin reads "is not gold."

Get it? "All that glitters is not gold."

# MAKING MONEY AT SEA

After the British colonies became the United States, shipping became an important industry, and many shipowners made millions. The richest of them owned whaling vessels. Profits on voyages ran from 100% to 300%, netting over $50,000 a trip.

For sailors, many of them teenagers, the story was different. At the end of each trip, they were paid from one-seventy-fifth to one-two-hundredth of the profit—or as little as the owner could get them to take.

Well, can you figure out what percentage one-two-hundredth is? How much would that come to if the owners made $75,000 a trip? How much would one-seventy-fifth of $75,000 be?

Look for the answer on page 35.

I got a job! $4.00 an hour to start and $5.00 an hour after six months.

Then why don't you start after six months?

Benjamin Franklin (1706–1790) was a ragged teenager when he started work as a printer in Philadelphia. But by the time he was forty-five years old, he was one of the richest men in America. Although Franklin preached thrift, he did not make his money by saving pennies. He imported printing presses from England, set them up in various colonies, and hired workers to run them. After a few years, the income from his shops was so great that he stopped working and devoted his time to his hobbies—science and diplomacy.

# CAN CHAIN LETTERS MAKE YOU RICH?

Thousands of dollars for only a dollar! That's what many chain letters promise. Some years ago Mrs. Susan Miller received one that made her very curious. There was no handwriting on it. It was just a typewritten page saying:

THIS CHAIN LETTER WORKS! THE CHAIN STARTED FOUR YEARS AGO AND HAS NEVER BEEN BROKEN

1. Tomorrow please send $1 to the first name on this list. Don't write a letter; just send a dollar.

2. Cross the first name off the list and put your name at the bottom of the list in the fifth place.

3. Make 5 copies of this letter with the new list. Mail it to 5 reliable people tomorrow.

4. Within 20 days your name will be first on 15,625 letters. Four days later you will receive $15,625.

   1. G. Armonk
      Perrysburg, Ohio 43155
   2. H.B. Pruitt
      Tenants Harbor, Maine 04860
   3. J.C. Thomas
      315 South Avenue
      New York, New York 10011

4. **M. Roman**
   **21 Hawthorne Circle**
   **New York, New York 10027**
5. **V. Lopez**
   **603 Circle Drive**
   **Portland, Oregon 97214**

Something must be wrong, Susan thought. The letter said she would get $15,625 twenty-four days after she sent a dollar to the first name on the list.

Susan knew the scheme wouldn't work. Yet she couldn't figure out what was the matter with it. Can you?

To begin with, the scheme would only work if everyone in the chain followed instructions.

And that's not likely to happen. But suppose the scheme worked? Let's say the mail takes 3 days. Four days after Susan mailed 5 copies of the letter with her name listed in the fifth place, 5 people would get it and if each sent out 5 copies to 5 people, 25 people would get it. In 8 days 5 × 25, or 125, people would get a copy with Susan's name fourth on the list. After 12 days 125 × 5, or 625, people would get a copy with her name in third place; after 16 days 625 × 5, or 3,125, would get a copy with her name in second place; after 20 days 3,125 × 5, or 15,625, would get a copy with her name in first place. Then, if each one mailed Susan $1, she would get $15,625. And how great that would be!

As Susan reread the chain letter, her eye fell on the statement that the chain had started four years earlier and never been broken. Could that be true, she wondered. She got out her calculator and began figuring out how many people would be in the chain if the number multiplied by 5 every 4 days. For 40 days, it would be $5 \times 5 \times 5 \times 5 \times 5 \times 5 \times 5 \times 5 \times 5 \times 5$, or 48,828,125. Continuing at that rate, after 52 days the number of people would be 6,103,515,625—over 6 billion. That's more than the entire population of the world!

What did Susan finally decide to do about the letter? She took a chance and followed the instructions.

What were the results? No one sent her a dollar.

Is the chain letter idea a scam? Not really. It is better described as a screwball scheme. When, where, and how the idea began is not known. But different forms of chain letters have been around for over two hundred years.

# THE BERRY PICKERS

Nowadays many states do not allow anyone under 18 to take a full-time job. But in Maine there are no rules for blueberry pickers. Since the crop is harvested in August when school is closed, many kids work as pickers. They are paid according to the number of baskets they pick. So the faster they work, the more they make.

One day Ronnie Hall set out to make lots of money as a picker. Starting with an empty basket, Ronnie worked slowly at first. Then he picked faster and faster, so that after every minute there were twice as many berries in the basket. In nine minutes, the basket was half full. How long did Ronnie take to fill the rest of it?

**Answer:** One minute. That's all it would take to double the amount already in the basket.

**Answers to Making Money at Sea:**

Since one-hundredth is 1%, one two-hundredth is half that, or .5%. And .5% of $75,000 is $375. That was poor pay, since whaling trips lasted for two or more years.

The sailor who got one-seventy-fifth of a profit of $75,000 was much better paid. He got $1,000.

Why was there such a great difference in pay? In whaling days, few sailors could handle fractions and many of them mistakenly thought a two-hundredth share was better than a seventy-fifth share. Of course, sailors only made that mistake on their first voyage. They learned arithmetic the hard way.

# BRAIN TICKLERS

1. **Suppose you have $1,000,000 and give away one quarter and another quarter and then another quarter. How much will you have left?**

2. **Who makes a million but is poorly paid?**

3. **A man had $35 in seven bills. Half of it was in $5 bills. What bills made up the other half?**

4. **What did the counterfeiter say when he was arrested?**

5. **On the basis of his data
   A steel dealer said he'd rather
   Sell 10,000 tons to Japan
   Than a single ton to Iran.
   Now what was the point of the matter?**

You can find the answers on page 38.

# POPCORN PROFITS

Lee, Dick, and Harry had been practicing magic tricks and were thinking of putting on a magic show to raise money for more equipment.

"I'd like to get the box you use to saw a girl in two and stick my sister in it," said Lee.

"Forget it. After you sawed her, she'd come out O.K. I'd rather have a high hat that you can pull a rabbit out of," said Dick.

"We can charge a quarter for admission," said Harry. "I'll take in the money and I'll make the coins vanish as I collect them. But will our friends pay money to see us? I think they'll only come for free. How can we get money out of them?"

"I know how," said Dick. "We can sell popcorn, like they do in the movies. You know you pay $3.00 for a bucket of popcorn that probably cost about a quarter. Why can't we do that kind of thing? Let's put on a free show at the Y and sell popcorn at the door."

And that's what the boys did. They bought 2 pounds of raw popcorn at the supermarket for $1.67, a bottle of corn oil for $1.13, and 200 paper cups for $1.00. Then they started experimenting. They learned there were 2½ cups of raw kernels in a pound and that each cup held 16 tablespoons. Using an electric popper, they got 2 cups of popcorn from 1 tablespoon of kernels, and that meant they could make lots of money selling popcorn by the cupful.

As it happened, a crowd turned out for the free show and every cup of popcorn was sold at a dime a cup. None was left for the boys. Harry was too busy to do his coin-vanishing act, but he didn't mind.

The boys were delighted with the money they made and you can see why. Figure out how much they took in from the sale of popcorn and the profit they made on it. Maybe you'll want to sell popcorn too.

How much did the boys take in? There were 2½ cups of kernels in a pound of raw popcorn, and the boys had bought 2 pounds. They started with 5 cups of kernels. Each cup held 16 tablespoons, and 1 tablespoon made 2 cups of popcorn. So the boys got 32 cups of popcorn from 1 cup of kernels. From 5 cups of kernels, they got 5 × 32, or 160 cups of popcorn. Selling the popcorn at 10¢ a cup, they took in $16.00. But that was not all profit. Their expenses were:

$1.67 raw popcorn
1.13 oil
1.00 cups
$3.80 total

After subtracting expenses from money taken in, the profit was:

$16.00
−3.80
$12.20 profit

"Wow!" said Harry, counting the money. "And we have half a bottle of oil left and about forty cups. Next time expenses will be lower and the profit higher. Say, when's our next show?"

# BUDDY'S BUSINESSES

Buddy wanted to earn money for a new TV game but wasn't sure how he could do it. When his cat had kittens, he tried selling them, but no one would pay money for them. So he gave the kittens away. When bluefish were running, he tried to sell his catch, but everybody else caught the fish too. So Buddy gave his catch to his mother. She was pleased but he wasn't, since he hated eating fish.

Then one day Buddy thought of going into the lawn-mowing business. His mother had a mower and there were plenty of lawns near his house that needed care.

His mother agreed to let him use the mower. "But, Buddy, you'll have to pay for the oil it burns. I've been paying eighty-one cents a quart for oil and I find a quart is enough for three lawns."

Buddy had no trouble getting customers. On Saturday he mowed two lawns in two hours in the morning and three lawns in two and a half hours in the afternoon. He charged $3 a lawn and felt great about all the money he made.

His big sister Claudia was unimpressed. "Subtract your expenses and figure out your average pay per hour. Then maybe you won't think you're so hot."

Just how much did Buddy make per hour?

**Answer:** Although Buddy took in $15 for mowing 5 lawns, he burned 1⅔ quarts of oil. That came to $.81 + $.54 = $1.35.

$15.00 income
− 1.35 expenses
$13.65 total earned

Since Buddy worked 4.5 hours, his average earning per hour was:

**$13.65 ÷ 4.5 = $3.03+**

Buddy was elated. "I think that's darn good pay," he said to Claudia. "I'm going to cut grass all year."

"Oh yeah?" said Claudia. "Grass doesn't grow in winter."

"So, I'll try cutting hair."

"With a lawn mower?"

# BUY, SELL OR SWAP

Looking for bargains began long before money was invented. People often bargained when they swapped things they had for things they wanted. Of course, swapping still goes on, but only on a small scale. Money made trading easier. It made bargain hunting easier, too.

# THE MANHATTAN ISLAND BARGAIN

The most valuable island in the world probably is Manhattan, the island that is now covered with New York City skyscrapers. Today the land on which those buildings stand is worth trillions and trillions of dollars. Yet back in 1626, when the island was covered with forest, a Dutch trading company bought it from Native Americans for the famous price of $24. Or so the company claimed.

Actually, no money was paid to the "wild men," as the Dutch called the Native Americans. The Dutch gave them trinkets valued at 60 guilder, which came to about $24 in English money. Since the Native Americans didn't use money when they traded, they were satisfied with the deal. In fact, they considered the trinkets a present because they didn't think that land could be bought and sold. As far as they were concerned, no one owned the land, and they continued to occupy it for almost a century.

Although Native Americans did not use money before Europeans arrived, some did use beads made from clams and periwinkles in trade with other tribes. These beads, called wampum, were woven into belts that were records of treaties or exchanges between tribes.

On learning how much wampum meant to the Native Americans, Europeans began to collect shells and trade them for skins of beaver and otter caught by the different tribes. And so wampum became a form of money.

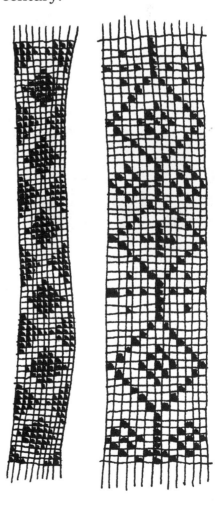

# SKIN DEAL

In the early days of the United States, trading with Native Americans for furs was an important business. Ships from Boston went on an eight-month voyage down the Atlantic coast, around the tip of South America, then up to the Pacific Northwest to obtain otter skins and other furs. In exchange, the Yankee traders offered trinkets, chisels, clothing, sheets of metal—anything they thought the Native Americans wanted.

Rates varied. In one place, a chisel was bartered for an otter skin; in another ten chisels bought one skin. But the value of a fine otter skin was fairly standard when otter skins were sold for money in China. There it was the favorite fur of many rulers. Skins shipped to them brought $50 apiece, according to old records.

One ship captain who traded with Native Americans noticed that some tribes used ermine skins as a form of money. On a voyage to Europe, where ermine was available, the captain bought 2,800 skins at a fair for 30¢ each. Then, on his next voyage to the Pacific Northwest, he bought 560 otter skins, paying 5 ermine skins for each one. Later he sold all 560 of them in China at $50 apiece.

What a deal! Can you figure out how much more was taken in on the sale of the otter skins than was paid for the ermine skins?

The answer is on page 44.

# COW TRADE— AFRICAN STYLE

In Kenya, in East Africa, barter was once the main means of trading. At one market, 1 hoe bought 3 chickens; 9 chickens bought 1 goat; 3 goats bought 1 cow.

How many chickens and goats would you need to buy 2 cows?

Look for the answer on page 44.

# JIMMY'S USED BIKE BUSINESS

Although it is easier to use money than to barter, records are important in figuring profit and loss. Since Jimmy was sloppy in keeping records, he was not always sure how he came out on a deal. Take this case. One day Jimmy sold a bike for $90, bought it back for $80 a week later, and then resold it for $100 the next day. So he thought he made $20 on the bike. Was his figuring correct?

**Answer:** Jimmy was $20 ahead when he resold the bike for $100 after buying it back for $80. But was that all he made on the bike? Jimmy really didn't know because he had forgotten how much he paid for it in the first place.

**Skin Deal Answer:** Since each ermine skin cost 30¢, 5 ermine skins cost $1.50, which was the price of a single otter skin. The price for 560 otter skins was 560 × $1.50 = $840. Since all 560 skins were sold at $50 apiece, the total taken in was 560 × $50 = $28,000. Subtract $840 from that and you get $28,000 − $840 = $27,160, which is how much more was taken in than was spent.

**Cow Trade Answer:** You could trade 3 goats for 1 cow, and since 9 chickens are worth 1 goat, you could trade 27 chickens for the other cow. You could also trade 2 goats and 36 chickens or 1 goat and 45 chickens.

# MAKING SENSE OUT OF PERCENT

P ercentages are a great help in doing business.

Since there are 100 cents to a dollar, a dealer who makes $.10 on a comic book that he sells for $1 makes a 10% profit on it. If he makes $.15 on the book, he makes a 15% profit, and so on.

Actually, 10% means 10/100, or .10, when written as a decimal. The figure 15% means 15/100, or .15. Any percentage can be changed into a decimal by multiplying it by .01. For example:

$$17\% = \frac{17}{100} = 17 \times .01 = .17$$

$$25\% = \frac{25}{100} = 25 \times .01 = .25$$

What does 100% equal? Multiply 100% by .01 and you get 1. So 100% of a dollar equals $1.00. How about 500% of a dollar? Since 500% × .01 = 5, it equals $5.00.

An easy way to handle percentages is to change them into decimals. With this in mind, can you figure out:

1. **What does 10,000% of $.01 equal?**

2. **What does 37½% of $3.00 equal?**

3. **If the price of a box of cereal costing $2.00 is raised 10% and then marked down 10%, will the price of the cereal be more, or less, than $2.00?**

**Answers:**
1. **10,000% × .01 = 100; 100 × $.01 = $1.00**

2. **37½% is the same as 37.5%. So 37.5 × .01 = .375; .375 × $3.00 = $1.125, or $1.13 rounded off.**

3. **Since 10% of $2.00 = $.20, that amount is added when the price of the cereal is raised, bringing it to $2.20. Ten percent of that comes to $2.20 × .1 = $.22. So when marked down, the new cereal price is $2.20 − $.22 = $1.98, which is lower than the original price.**

# PROFIT OR LOSS?

The Otto family was about to move from New York to California. They had two cars which they decided to sell instead of driving them across the continent. Although the cars were not new when purchased, both were in good condition and Mr. Otto was able to sell them for $3,000 each. On one car, he made a profit of 20%; on the other, he took a loss of 20%.

Can you figure out how he came out on the sale of the two cars? Did he make or lose money or did he break even?

**Answer:**

The $3,000 taken in when making a profit of 20% was 120% of the purchase price. To find that price, change 120% into a decimal and divide $3,000 by it: $3,000 ÷ 1.2 = $2,500. The 20% profit on that was $2,500 × .2 = $500.

The $3,000 taken in when losing 20% was 80%, or .8 of the price of the second car. That car cost $3,000 ÷ .8 = $3,750 and the loss on it was $3,750 − $3,000 = $750.

Together the two cars cost $3,750 + 2,500 = $6,250. And that was more than the $6,000 Mr. Otto paid for them.

# THE PRESIDENT'S HORSE

This is based on a true story about President Ulysses S. Grant and his favorite horse, Butcher Boy.

One day when the President was on his way back to the White House in his horse and carriage, he was passed on the road by a butcher cart. "The horse pulling it went so fast, he made my team seem to be standing still," said Grant to his aide. "Find out who owns the horse and buy him for me, if the owner will sell."

The owner was quite happy to part with the horse and sold Butcher Boy for $220, which was half the price he would have asked had he known the President was buying him.

Grant also bought a mate for the horse, which his wife rode. They became fond of their horses and frequently rode them around Washington.

After leaving the White House, Grant ran into financial trouble

and put the horses up for auction. The two were sold for the sum of $493.68. Grant was very disappointed. He had expected the horses would bring much more than that.

"Anyway," said Mr. Reed, the auctioneer. "You came out ahead. You made a profit of twelve percent on Butcher Boy's mate, although you lost ten percent on him. So you made two percent."

"Did you say two percent? That only comes to nine dollars and sixty-eight cents, the way I figure it," said Grant.

"Sorry, sir," said Mr. Reed. "The figures are correct."

Were they? Had Mr. Reed made an error?

(Hint: First find out the cost of the two horses.)

**Answer:**

The profit of 2% was based on the cost of both horses. Since that was $9.68, 1% was half that, or $4.84. The cost of both horses was 100 times that, or $484.

Butcher Boy cost $220, so his mate cost $484 − $220 = $264.

A profit of 12%, or .12, was made on her. That came to $264 × .12 = $31.68.

The loss of 10% on Butcher Boy who had cost $220 came to $220 × .1 = $22.

Subtract the loss from the profit and you get $31.68 − $22 = $9.68.

So Mr. Reed's figures were correct.

# ROUNDING UP, ROUNDING DOWN

Rounding, as you know, is a way of writing a number or an amount of money so it ends in zero. A sum such as $1.02 can be rounded down to $1.00; $1.19 can be rounded up to $1.20. As a rule, the sum is changed to one that can be divided by ten. This makes the handling of money much easier.

How do you know when to round up and when to round down? Of course, there is no problem if the last digit is 0. But if it is 1, 2, 3, or 4, that digit is changed to 0. If the last digit is 5, 6, 7, 8, or 9, the preceeding digit is rounded up, so that the last digit is 0. As a result, $.25 becomes $.30; $4.69 becomes $4.70.

After your family has shopped at a supermarket, take the slip from the cash register and round off every amount on it, then get the total. When you compare that total with the one on the slip, you probably will find very little difference between them.

In making an estimate, it's helpful to round prices to the nearest dollar. Say you have a clothing allowance of $100 and you need a jacket, jeans, a sweater, two shirts, sneakers, and socks. Would it be better to round prices down, or up, to the nearest dollar to make sure you have enough money for your purchases?

**Answer:** Rounding downward would mean you expect to pay less than the actual prices. So, in making an estimate, it's wise to round prices upward.

# SPORTY TRADING CARDS

In your parents' and grandparents' day, baseball cards were given away free in packs of bubble gum. In fact, specks of gum can still be found on many of the old freebies. Today, old cards are collectors' items and catalogs listing prices for them often give two figures—the price for a card that had gum on it and the price for a spotless one. In some cases, the prices run into hundreds of dollars.

Gone are the days of free trading cards. New ones are generally sold in packs of 15 and adults as well as kids collect and swap them. Fast thinking is often needed in making deals, as these problems show:

1. Jeff had a pack of 15 baseball cards worth $1.50, another pack worth $2.00 and one worth $2.50. Rocky had a pack of 15 cards worth $3.00, and wanted to trade with Jeff. How many cards from each of Jeff's packs would be a fair trade for Rocky's pack?

2. If a pack of baseball cards plus one extra card cost $1.24, and the pack costs $1.00 more than the extra card, what does the pack cost?

3. A price war is going on between two dealers who sell the same cards. One marks his cards down 25%. Then the other dealer marks his cards down 40%. To compete, the first dealer further reduces his prices 15%. Who offers the better buy?

Answers:
1. The boys figured that Jeff's cards were each worth:
$1.50 ÷ 15 = $.10 from pack 1
$2.00 ÷ 15 = $.133, or $.13 rounded, from pack 2
$2.50 ÷ 15 = $.166, or $.17 rounded, from pack 3
If Rocky took ten from each of Jeff's packs, he would have

cards worth
$1.00 + $1.33 + $1.67 = $4.00. But since Rocky's pack was worth only $3.00, they figured out the value of eight cards from each pack. They found:
8 × $.10 = $ .80
8 × $.13 = $1.04
8 × $.17 = $1.36
  total = $3.20, which was $.20 too much.
  So Jeff said, "How about 6 ten-cent cards and 8 thirteen-cent cards and 8 seventeen-cent cards? And you can pick the ones you want."
  "Okay," said Rocky. "It's a deal."

2. Since the pack is $1.00 more than the pack and extra card costing $1.24, the extra card cost $.12, and the pack cost $1.12.

3. Let's say the original price of a pack is $1.00. Take 25% of that and you get $1.00 × .25 = $.25, subtract it from $1.00 and you get $1.00 − $.25 = $.75. Take 15% of that and you will get $.75 × .15 = $.1125, which rounds to $.11. Then subtract $.75 − $.11 = $.64. And that's the marked down price.

  Well, 40% of $1.00 is $.40, which subtracted from $1.00 gives $1.00 − $.40 = $.60. And that's the better bargain.
  Try a 40% markdown on any price and you'll find it's always better than a 25% markdown followed by one of 15%.

# PRICE CODES

**N**early all packaged goods bought at supermarkets are marked with bar codes. These codes are patterns of wide and narrow black lines with spaces between and numerals at the bottom. When an item goes to the checkout counter, the pattern is placed on a part called a scanner, which is connected to a computer. One part of the pattern stands for the selling price of the item. After the computer decodes the price, it is flashed on the screen of the cash register. Other parts of the bar code pattern contain information that is stored in the computer's memory for later use.

To the left of the bar code block is a numeral that classifies the item. For instance, 0 stands for something from the grocery department. Next comes a group of five digits that identifies the maker or source of the product. The next group of five digits

indicates details such as size and contents.

Perhaps the manager of your local supermarket will explain the system in greater detail to a group from your class.

Many smaller stores that do not have registers with scanners indicate the cost of items on price tags by using a code. The code is based on a word having ten letters, each of which stands for one of the ten digits.

Say a store is using the code word *symbolized,* and S = 1, Y = 2, M = 3, and so on. Then the cost of SMOD would be $13.50. If the price tag read $27.00, you would know the store is charging $13.50 more than the item cost and the markup was 100%.

How much did an item marked LEZ cost? If the price tag read $9.77, what was the percentage of the markup? And what was the cost of an item marked MYB? If the selling price was $6.48, what was the percentage of the markup?

**Answers:**

The key word is
S Y M B O L I Z E D
Each letter stands for one digit:
1 2 3 4 5 6 7 8 9 0

So LEZ cost $6.98. If $9.77 was the selling price, the markup was $9.77 − $6.98 = $2.79. The percentage of the markup was $2.79 ÷ $6.98 = .399, or 40%.

MYB cost $3.24. The selling price was $6.48. So the markup was $6.48 − $3.24 = $3.24, which is 100% above the cost.

# FLEA MARKET ARITHMETIC

Lakeside Flea Market
Saturday, June 30
Sell Stuff Yourself or
Let Chuck Ross Sell It For You
COME ONE, COME ALL!

Announcements had been posted all over town and lots of people showed up. Several kids came with money to spend and a few came with things to sell.

Nancy and Sharon had three trays of homemade fudge, cut into squares, which they were selling at 10¢ apiece. They did not expect any change problems, and started with nine coins that came to $1.09.

Their first customer said that before he could buy anything, he needed change for a half dollar. Nancy checked the change box and said, "Sorry, we can't change it."

Then the man asked if they had change for a quarter. Again the answer was no. The girls couldn't even change a nickel.

What coins did the girls have?

**Answer:**

Since the girls had $1.09 in coins, four were pennies. The other five were a half dollar, a quarter and three dimes.

Barry and Sid both grew and sold tomatoes. They decided to have a merger and sell together at the Flea Market. A week earlier Barry had sold 30 tomatoes at three for $1.00 and taken in $10.00, while Sid had sold 30 at two for $.85 and taken in $12.75. Together they had made $22.75. In pricing their tomatoes for the Flea Market, they figured three for $1.00 plus two for $.85 made five for $1.85. So they decided to sell their tomatoes at $.37 each.

The day of the Flea Market the boys sold 60 tomatoes at $.37 each and took in $22.20, instead of $22.75, as in the previous week. What had happened to that extra $.55?

**Answer:**

The boys were charging their customers too little. Barry's tomatoes had been selling for $.333 each, while Sid's were selling for $.425 each. Their average price was

$.333 + $.425 ÷ 2 = $.379

That's $.38 rounded, which was

about a cent too low.

Caroline brought an old radio to Chuck Ross, hoping he would sell it. He told her, "Put the selling price on the radio. After I sell it, I'll take one-fourth off for my work and give you the rest. So price the radio one-third higher than what you want to get for it."

Caroline wanted to get $7.50 for the radio, and after adding ⅓ to $7.50, she priced it at $10.00. When Chuck sold it, he took ¼ off as his pay, which came to $2.50. Caroline got $7.50 for the radio, but she couldn't figure out why the system worked. Can you?

**Answer:** By adding ⅓ to the desired price, the selling price becomes 4/3 of it. Multiply that by ¼, which is Chuck's pay, and you get ⅓: $4/3 \times 1/4 = 1/3$. Neat, isn't it?

# ANYTHING WRONG HERE?

**Maybe there is and maybe there isn't. That's why these brain teasers are ticklers and, in some cases, mind-stretchers.**

## THE SMART IDIOT

According to an old folktale, people often showed the village idiot two coins—a nickel and a dime—then told him he could have whichever one he preferred. Invariably, the boy chose the nickel, and villagers laughed, thinking he chose it because it was bigger.

One day a kind old lady took the boy aside and said, "Folks are just teasing you with that nickel-dime business. I'm going to put an end to it."

"Oh, don't do that," said the idiot. People would stop asking me which coin I wanted if I chose the dime."

Moral: Be careful how you answer questions. What may seem to be a dumb choice could be the smart one.

## OH, O. HENRY

An interesting counting problem appears in a famous story, "The Gift of the Magi," written around 1900 by O. Henry, a popular American author of the time. The story is about a young couple who is broke, yet they want to buy Christmas presents for each other. The husband has sold his gold watch in order to buy a set of fancy combs that his wife can use for her lovely long hair. Meanwhile, his wife decides to have her hair cut and sell the hair to buy a watch chain for her husband.

The story begins:

"One dollar and eighty-seven cents. That was all. And sixty of it was in pennies. Pennies saved one and two at a time . . . Three

times Della counted it. One dollar and eighty-seven cents. And the next day would be Christmas.''

Check Della's arithmetic and you wonder if she could count. But the author insists the sum she arrives at is correct.

Literary critics have pointed out that O. Henry was often a sloppy writer and that accounts for the figures he used in the story. Check them yourself and it does seem that O.Henry made a mistake. But did he? Was there any way, at the time, to get $1.87 using sixty pennies?

**Answer:** In addition to $.60, Della needed $1.27. That could have been made up without any pennies, for a 3-cent piece was in circulation at the time. This coin was introduced to help people make change after the Civil War,

when there was a coin shortage. Besides nickels, dimes, and quarters to make up a dollar, Della might have had nine 3-cent pieces, or some other combination using that coin.

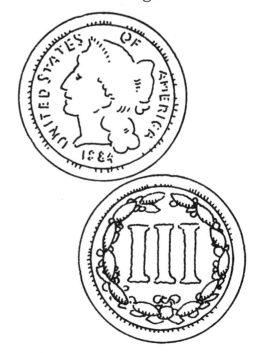

# MIKE'S BIKE

**M**ike wanted a new bike—one that cost $100. But he knew his parents were hard up and that he would have to earn the money himself. The prospects for that were slim, since jobs for teenagers were scarce.

Mike was about to give up hope of getting a new bike when Joey told him that 1977 nickels were worth about $100. "Boy, oh boy!" said Mike, "There must be lots of 1977 nickels around. The bike is mine."

Said Joey, "Don't count on it." Now, why did he say that?

**Answer:** A nickel is worth 5¢, isn't it? So 1977 × 5¢ = $98.85, which is about $100.00.

# FINAL MARKDOWN

**G**ladys saw an add in the paper announcing:

ADDITIONAL **25%** OFF ALL SWEATERS THAT HAVE ALREADY BEEN REDUCED BY **50%** !!

"Hey, Ma, now you can get me that classy forty-dollar sweater I want at twenty-five percent plus fifty percent off. That's seventy-five percent off—and that adds up to a thirty-dollar saving! The sweater will cost only ten dollars!"

"No, Gladys," said her mother. "The sweater will be more than that. Your math is all wrong."

What was the final price of the sweater?

**Answer:** After the first markdown of 50%, the price of the $40 sweater was $20. An additional 25% off would bring the price down to $15.

# THE DAUGHTERS' QUARTERS

**B**efore leaving the house, Mrs. Smith took four quarters from her purse, put them on the table, and told her three daughters to divide the money among themselves so that each sister would have no more than either of the others.

The oldest daughter took charge and, without making change, divided the money as her mother had instructed.

How was that possible?
**Answer:** The oldest gave herself two quarters, then gave each of her sisters one quarter. When they protested, she pointed out that neither of them had more than the other two, although she herself had more than *either* of them. Then she added, "Anyway, Mom didn't say the money had to be divided evenly."

# THE WHOLE HOLE

**T**he gang boss who was hiring ditch diggers wanted to be sure they could handle figures and measurements correctly. So he made up a simple test. He asked this question: If two people get $20 for digging a hole that's 4 feet deep, 3 feet wide, and 4 feet long—a hole that's 48 cubic feet—how much should they be paid for digging half a hole? Most men answered $10. But those men were never hired. Why?
**Answer:** There's no such thing as half a hole. A hole is a whole . . . always.

# THE CASE OF THE MISSING MONEY

**T**hree men checked in at a motel in the late afternoon and each took a separate room. The clerk charged them $30 apiece, receiving $90 for the three rooms.

In the evening the manager noticed that the men had been overcharged. The regular rate for each room was $25. To straighten things out, he called a bellhop, gave him the extra $15 that had been collected, and told him to return the overcharge due each man.

The bellhop, who wasn't as honest as he should be, gave each man only $3. Then he kept the rest for himself, which came to $6. Now, each man, instead of paying $30 for his room, paid $27. For the three rooms they paid $81, but since the bellhop had pocketed $6, that added up to $87. What happened to the other $3?
**Answer:** No money was missing. Two separate business deals took place. In one the motel collected $90 and then deducted $15, which was the overcharge. As a result, the amount taken in was

$75. In the other deal, each man actually paid $27 for his room. From that, subtract the $2 pocketed by the bellhop and $25 is left. Multiply $25 by three and you get $75, the final amount taken in by the motel.

# PEWEE'S BOAST

Pewee was shorter than his friends, which was the reason for his nickname. "Don't worry about it," said his father. "You'll get a spurt of growth in a year or so and catch up with the rest of your friends. That happened to me. I used to be a teenage dwarf, but now I'm over six feet. You'll get there, too. And if not, so what? The main thing is to be physically fit and strong."

The word "strong" appealed to Pewee and so he went in for weight lifting. But building up his arm and shoulder muscles was taking too long. He didn't want to admit this, and announced that he was working on his hands. "They're now so strong," Pewee boasted, "I can pick up ten pounds of pennies with just one hand."

When his friends asked for a demonstration, Pewee did what he claimed he could do. How did he do it?

**Answer:** First Pewee emptied a penny bank and formed a mound with the coins. "I don't know exactly how much all these pennies weigh, but they weigh a lot. Anyone want to try to pick them all up with one hand?" When no one volunteered, Pewee said, "Well, watch me." And using only his right hand, Pewee picked up all the pennies—a few at a time.

# CHALLENGES, CHALLENGES

1. How can you fold a half dollar?

2. Ask a friend to shake some coins from a piggy bank and pick them up without showing you how many he or she is holding. Then you shake the bank and do the same, saying, "Bet I have more money in my hand than you do." You're sure to win. How come?

3. Can you explain this?

   There was a young man from Newgate,
   Who stood on an orange crate.
   If you stuck a penny on his forehead,
   He would get a look that was horrid.
   Then, without seeing the penny,
   Would tell you the date.

4. Put nine pennies down on the table, then remove four of them. Add three nickels, and you'll have seven coins worth 19¢. Can you do it?

5. Tell your friends to take all the dimes they have and lay them heads down on a table. Then offer to pay a nickel for every dime whose date you can't name, sight unseen. The more dates you fail to guess, the more money you will collect. Can you figure out why?

Answers

1. Fold a dollar bill in half and then fold that half.

2. **You win because your friend won't have any money in your hand—not a single cent.**

3. **You can do the trick, too. Have someone stick a penny on your forehead without showing you the coin. You pretend to do some hard thinking and say, "I am sure the date is—" and then you name the present year.**

4. **Take four pennies from the nine on the table. Set the four aside, add the three nickels to them, and you have seven coins worth 19¢. Simple, isn't it? But most people try to add the nickels to five of the nine pennies.**

5. **Each time you pick up a dime, you give a nickel in return for it, if you fail to guess the date on the dime. So you make 5¢ for each mistake, and the more mistakes you make, the more money you collect.**

# ARITHMETRICK

To encourage her daughter Maria in doing her math homework, Mrs. Ortiz offered to pay Maria 8¢ for every problem she got right and to fine her 5¢ for every problem she got wrong. After 26 problems, neither one owed anything to the other. How many problems did Maria solve correctly?

**Answer:** The trick in figuring out the answer is to realize that when Maria gets 1 problem right and 1 problem wrong, she earns 3¢. When she gets 10 right and 10 wrong, she earns 30¢. But after 20 problems, there are 6 more to go. If Maria gets all 6 problems wrong, she will have to pay her mother 30¢, canceling what she had earned. So with 10 right and 16 wrong, neither one owes anything to the other.

# GOLDEN OLDIE

**T**his one is over 150 years old but it's still good:

Four jolly men sat down to play,
And played all night to early day,
They played for cash, not for fun,
Yet when they squared accounts,
All had made fair amounts.
Now here is something to explain:
If no one lost, how could all gain?

**Answer:**
The men were fiddlers
Who played all night
Giving dancers great delight.
When morning came,
Each went away
With the cash that was his pay.

# TAX PROBLEM

**E**ach year the owner of the Eagle Tool Company bought 1,000 tons of steel. The steel was made into tools, which were sold at a profit. Usually, the owner made $250,000. This went on year after year, but neither the company nor the owner ever paid the United States government a cent of income tax. How come?
**Answer:** The owner was a Canadian and Eagle Tool was a Canadian company.

# TRUE OR FALSE?

**F**or years there has been a rumor that the United States issued a special $1 bill to mark the assassination of President Kennedy. This bill bears the date 1963, the year Kennedy was shot, and the number 11 appears on it four times because the president was assassinated in November, the eleventh month of the year, and it carries the words "Dallas, Texas," the city in which the killing took place. It also has a large letter *K* within a circle and in front of each serial number.

It is true there is such a $1 bill, but does that bill have any connection with Kennedy's death?

**Answer:** None of the markings on the dollar have anything to do with Kennedy's death. The date 1963 shows that it is one of a series issued in that year and the letter *K* shows that the Dallas Federal Reserve issued it. The number 11 appears on the bill because the bank is in the 11th Federal Reserve District, and the words "Dallas, Texas" are on all Federal Reserve notes issued by that bank.

# STRANGE HARDWARE

n a hardware store, not so long ago, a customer asked how much a certain item would cost. When the clerk said 10¢, the customer asked how much 12 would cost and the answer was 20¢. The customer then said he needed 112 and the clerk said that would cost 30¢.

What in the world was the customer buying?

**Answer:** The man lived at 112 Star Lane and was buying a new set of house numbers.

1963, THE YEAR KENNEDY WAS SHOT.

11, SIGNIFYING THE MONTH OF NOVEMBER.

K, FOR KENNEDY, AND DALLAS, WHERE THE KILLING TOOK PLACE

# WEIGHTY MATTER

**W**hen is a $100 bill equal to a $1 bill?

**Answer:** When you weigh them. A $100 bill and a $1 bill weigh 1 gram each. Take our word for it, since it's not likely that you can lay your hands on a $100 bill and compare it with a $1 bill.

Even with coins, the most weight doesn't always mean the most value. A penny and a dime both weigh 2½ grams, while a nickel weighs 5 grams.

# BIG FEET, LITTLE FEET

**F**ootprints had been taken of all the children in P.S. 52. Then the school was given an arithmetic test that included a lot of money problems. Later, test scores were compared with the footprints, and the results showed that the children with big feet were better at solving the problems than those with small feet. Was something wrong with the test?

**Answer:** Probably not. As a rule, children with big feet are older than those with little feet, and so they are better at handling money problems.

# INDEX

Anthony, Susan B., 21

Bank book, 26
Bank loans, 26
Bar codes, 50
Barter, 42
Baseball cards, 48
Bureau of Engraving and
    Printing, 19, 20

Cents, 6
Chain letters, 33
Change, 16
Coins, 7
Colonies, 10
Copper, 7, 8, 11
Counterfeit coins, 11–12
Counterfeits, 21
Credit card, 25, 26

Decimal money system, 10
Decimals, 10
Denver, 8
Dime, 10
*Disme*, 10
Dollar, silver, 21–22
Dollars, 17–22

Ermine skins, 42
Estimate, 47

Federal Reserve, 19
Federal Reserve Banks, 20
Franklin, Benjamin, 31, 33

Gasparro, Frank, 7
"The Gift of the Magi", 54
Gold rush, 29
Grant, Ulysses, S., 46

Interest, 24
Interest rates, 26

Kennedy, President, 61
Kenya, 43

*La Disme*, 10
Lincoln Memorial, 6
Loan shark, 27
Loss, 45

Markdown, 56
Milling, 11
Mint, 8

Native Americans, 41

Pennies, 6
Percent, 27
Percentages, 44
Philadelphia, 8
*Poor Richard's Almanac*, 31
Pounds, 10
Printing, money, 20
Profit, 36, 45

Rounding down, 47
Rounding up, 47

Shillings, 10
Shipping, 32

Tatum, Josh, 11
Trading, 48
Treasury Department, 21

Wampum, 41
Washington, George, 19
Weight, 8–9
White House, 46

Yen, 22